Drive-By Vigils

Drive-By Vigils

R. Zamora Linmark

Hanging Loose Press
Brooklyn, New York

Published by Hanging Loose Press, 231 Wyckoff Street, Brooklyn, New York, 11217-2208. www.hangingloosepress.com. All Rights Reserved. No part of this book may be reproduced without the publisher's written permission, except for brief quotations in reviews.

Printed in the United States of America
10 9 8 7 6 5 4 3 2 1

Hanging Loose Press thanks the Literature Program of the New York State Council on the Arts for a grant in support of the publication of this book.

Cover art: *School Service* by Elmer Borlongan, oil on canvas, 153 cm x 153 cm, courtesy of Dr. Joven Cuanang and the Pinto Art Museum

Cover design by Marie Carter

Library of Congress Cataloging-in-Publication Data available on request.

CONTENTS

for Faye Kicknosway

&

Lisa Asagi, Justin Chin, and Lori Takayesu

I

HAMLET REDUX

If *Hamlet* were up to me, I'd trade his sword
for a yoga mat, shift his suicide-sprinkled
soliloquy from Denmark to the Middle East,
then give the Prince of Paranoia backstage
tips on chat room protocol. On line, he'll waste
no time in spilling out to voyeurs and
masturbators his woes, wants, and frozen
desires for his wannabe girlfriend Ophelia,
who, from the get-go, suspects him
of playing mind games. After squabbling
over a missed call from a guy named Bob,
she drops his ass off at the nearest cemetery
then, before speeding off forever, thanks
him for saving her from an unnecessary drowning,
giving her the chance to bank on her dream
of becoming a Korean karaoke bar rap artist.
In this NC-17 version, there will be lots of anti-
psychotic pills, compulsive heterosexual-
themed balls with matching gowns and pyro-
technics, one or two raunchy panic attack scenes
between an insomniac Hamlet and his best friend
Horatio, cruise missile shows, mass butcherings,
child labor law offenses, a giant talking
condom as King Hamlet's ghost, and surprise
cameos by George Bush Sr. & Jr. as
opening acts for Rosencrantz & Guildenstern.
Gertrude will be granted a one-night stand
in the bombed city of her choosing, but her lover
Claudius, Hamlet's uncle, will end up dead
smack in the center of a minefield. Drama
slightly altered to fit into today's madness,
but the movement from grief to grand descent
to the inevitable fatal finale I'm sticking with
just for old time's sake.

Twelve Short Takes on Montgomery Clift

Take 1

Acting is an accumulation
of subtleties—like shaking the ash
from a cigarette while you
are supposed to be completely
absorbed in a conversation.

Take 2

How does it feel to be dead?
Start with the face.
Left side paralyzed.
Teeth knocked out.
Jaws wired shut.
And he was not even drunk or high
when he slammed right
into the mountain.

Take 3

Counterclockwise.
Begin with: "Absolutely not."
Monty's last words
recorded at one in the morning—
a response to his Negro caregiver
who asked if he cared
to catch himself on the tube
controlling his temper
inside a phone booth

in the middle of the desert,
his half-drowned words blaming
his mother's second marriage
for robbing him of his ranch inheritance
then shrugging at the word "home"
and the mention of scars healing on his face.

Take 4

"Please don't wake me when I'm smoking."

Take 5

Clockwise. End with
the making of *The Misfits*,
when Monty, born fifteen hours
behind his twin sister Esther,
is asking the same question
as forty years ago:
"Did I begin like her?"

Take 6

Gossip columnist Hedda Hopper: "In one sentence, what is the story of
your life?"

Monty: "I've been knifed."

Take 7

"Dear K—

        Why is it that nothing

I ever write in a letter makes sense—
Silence—

        always silence—
How to fill it up—And with what—
but more silence.

        Yours, with a limp,

        Monty."

Take 8
(Or: "A Short History of a Throat.")

Before Monty turned ten, he'd crossed the Atlantic
enough times to forget chewing gum
and the World Series.
        Once, aboard the *Isle of France,*
a boy tried to drown him in the pool.
This left him with a busted gland
and a scar on his neck, unlike the ones
children get from the throat of *Printemps.*
        From a window
above 125 Rue St. Michel, he studied
culture and other nuances. By nineteen,
he'd had enough of Proust's madeleines
and Thomas Mann's *Death* in Deutsch.

Take 9

Observe death in Latin.
Avoid pills and blackouts.
Extend sleep until four in the morning.
Lie between a kiss and a killer's confession.
Spend two days saying, "Who's that?" to a prostitute.
Portray life as if it were your last sorrow.

Take 10

After one take, a last meal: Goose liver sandwich.

Take 11

Marilyn and Monty: Revelation scene:
A saloon outside Dayton, Nevada.
Everywhere flies swarming amidst black tarps.
Day for night.
Marilyn holding water in a paper cup.
Monty sipping vodka-spiked juice.
Between takes: they compared paranoia and pill list,
shared strategies for combating insomnia,
the location of their loneliness.
According to Monty, it was in Marilyn's smile.
According to Marilyn, it was in Monty's laugh.

Epilogue

 "That goddamn fag," Gable,
standing on a dry lake, said,
"just stole the scene from me
by lighting that cigarette."

COMFORT

for Mark Pawlak

Forget the first sun in three weeks
I'm starting to get used to imagining
Bukowski's beer and ashtray breath
on my crotch, the infamous bulbous nose,
deep grooves on the forehead and
around the spit-moistened lips,
the beard of a cave-dwelling saint,
pink, hairy moles sprouting on acne scars

The verses I hate to admit
are turning me on, cheap
lines about three-dollar Mexican putas,
passive-aggressive Japanese girlfriends,
lost weekends totaling ten blackout years

This recovering alcoholic never tires
of absorbing and recounting
his thin long poems about polyps,
in-your-face pussy-eating contests,
his homages to the homos
I love and look up to, like
Tchaikovsky who was better off
composing than faking orgasm
with his diva crazier than him,
Lorca who filled his odes
with olives, moon, matadors,
Crane who swam into a boat's
propeller after he popped the question
to a woman, and, if fag hag counts,
Carson McCullers, fluent
in the gay lingua of Goth and camp

The collection is not complete without
the master expounding on the art of
plucking the nosehair of forgiveness,
bragging how he went from well
to hell with one shot of agave tequila,
giving tips to cabin-fevered poets on
what they should do when love opens again

all kinds of loneliness: Let the tigers
of the past lie next to us, let them lick
all our hours of vulgar comfort
while we stroke their fur—ashes now—
still fierce to drive out the best day
of the year to a remarkable start.

Turning Forty-One

Magic number for popping polyps,
Flaring up, changing slogans.

Art for arthritis' sake.
Here's to a fabulous fibrous future.

Mid-life, mid-mark, midway—
What's to calculate?

Japan will always be older by a year.
Guam by half a day.

Let the Battle of the Bulge
And Midriff Blues begin.

Don't despair.
Here, have a cup of crushed ice.

Warm up the search engine.
Today marks the eighth chance.

With or without a waiver,
Proceed as usual.

Brake only for ordinary
Voices of saints, counting

Forty full years endlessly
To sleep.

First Known: A Study of Compound Words Beginning With "After"

from the "First Known Use" *section of the Merriam Webster Dictionary website*

Six years separate "afterbirth" from "afterlife"
and I was made to believe
"afternoons" began in the 14th century.
"Afterwards"—nothing, until grass grew
two hundred years later.
It's what happens in an "aftermath": you lose
track of the candle maker. Then you
wait for another three hundred fifty years
for something like an "afterglow."

But there are some things to be thankful for,
like the 17th century for introducing "afterthought,"
like surviving the "aftershock" of 1894,
like letting go of "afterwit" as of 1578.

Sunday Morning

Thank god the winds return from
a week ago to carry me back
to San Telmo where men stood
on cobblestones holding up signs
for free hugs I made full use of
until I saw the most memorable part
thus far of this journey a woman
surfacing from a story she held
in the palm of her hands awe
and contentment fueled her gaze
as if she had just returned from
the greatest drowning of her life
to say I will never be as happy as
where these words have taken me.

Found in Palermo, Buenos Aires

Craving Borges, after Bolaño's *Romantic*
Dogs and Puig's *Heartbreak Tango*,
I take a subway ride to Palermo,
alight at Thames, pass an old woman
dusting off a rug on El Salvador,
shouting, Cuidado, cuidado! at me
because dog shit sticks, even in our sleep,
so I check the soles of my shoes
before turning onto Nicaragua,
"La Javanaise" in my head, until
Gainsbourg gets sidetracked
by a whistling train at Honduras,
its station of sad faces I cover up quickly
with Manila scenes and soundtracks
because Manila can't stand silence
and sadness that, sooner or later,
catches up no matter how calm
or close we are to happiness, so
I run fast along Panama, take refuge
in a rundown café, and wait on
my Borges con leche.

ANOTHER NIGHTMARE

in which
I am the hero

stuck
in a war.

There are others, too.
"Fucking murderers!"

she calls us,
whoever *she* is.

That's when I stand up
and give a speech

I will never remember.
Still,

it comes loud
and clear enough

to hear my words
in somebody else's voice.

I wake up, searching
the darkness for scraps—

the accumulation of evidence
passing for Hell:

phantom soldiers craving
the sound of church bells,

madmen resurrecting
childhood corpses,

reunions with abandoned
memories.

Rather die
than dream again,

I get down
on my knees, and,

like a poet,
bargain with Him

who, for once,
is not missing

or does not
miss His cue.

"Go back
to sleep," He says,

"Trust me."
which I

mishear as
"Try me."

AFTER PESSOA

Today's rain takes over this city
& my mind gathers everything
about beauty & all that it clutters
so what mattered once
again matters and I become the student:
Whose ghost do I return to here?
To whom do I owe this honor of
the necessary disquietude I keep
tricking myself into believing
is mine to name and unmake?

Some Kind of Wonderful

for John Hughes, American Filmmaker: 1950-2009

I wanted to save my dandruff for winter.

I wanted the school's most-wanted truant to give me his stud earring then
     French kiss me in the library.

I wanted my heart to break out and lip-synch to "Try a Little Tenderness."

I wanted Psychedelic Furs to accompany my pink, beat-up imaginary
     Karmann Ghia to the Senior Prom.

I drove a secondhand white Ford Escort.

I gave my prom date a Swatch watch in lieu of a corsage.

I was scared straight-acting at the time.

I wanted the auto mechanic to run after my tears.

I wanted him to kiss me on the wrong side of the tracks.

I twice made out on the right side of track and field.

"I am not a nymphomaniac, I am a compulsive liar."

I reserved high-intensity feelings for dickheads in Izods and low ones for
     waistoids in Fred Perrys and Sperry Topsiders.

I was a dweeb with a staple gun to my heart.

I wanted to eat John Bender's shorts.

I mohawked my mornings in the shower.

I was mistaken once for a lesbian drummer.

I wanted red highlights, silver studs on my leather shoes, a truant's
     crucifix earring.

I never had my hairy butt duct-taped by a wrestler.

No way would I sacrifice a Saturday to tell you who you are.

I was poor, I was fashion conscious, I was Goodwill incarnate.

I wanted a rich, hypochondriac, son-of-a-Ferrari-freak for a sidekick.

I wanted to conquer the ballroom with a bland guy named Blane.

I wanted to be some kind of wonderful to my toupee-wearing band
     teacher.

I wanted the principal to hound me like a second shadow.

I wanted Ben Stein as my Economics teacher.

"Bueller . . . Bueller . . . Bueller."

But my high school could only afford a part-time Social Studies teacher.

S.S. was Econ on welfare.

I wanted to pretend I was Sausage King of the Windy City.

I wanted to be geek, jock, basket case, prom queen, criminal.

I wanted all of the above.

Until I realized I was—throwing confetti on Chicago and singing "Danke
     Schoen" on a magnificent-mile-long float.

Danke Schoen, John Hughes, Danke Schoen.

Postscript

I am embarrassed to report
that the world,
as you predicted,
is losing the war.

As of today,
despite heartbreaking
months of breaking open
mountains & deserts,

recovering
only a warehouse
of unwanted footage
from old MGM musicals,

pesticides
of mass destruction
remain a mystery
near Mesopotamia.

I am pleased,
however,
to announce that
the cows,

as you predicted,
continue to graze
& are at peace
with their Moo

rich on chicken
manure &
Spring's last-
minute blossoms.

A True Account of Talking to a Coqui Frog at Reed Island, Hilo

for Jaime Jacinto

Those damn frogs won't let me sleep.
They're up in the trees, croaking:

"Eh, Chico, you no can pass out yet.
You barely wrote one line."

"After five sleepless nights
Why only now?"

"Be grateful.
The buggah down the street one poet too."

"He's half-dead
and only writes in Russian."

"Us got interpreters. They just on furlough
Friday, Saturday, Sunday, Monday, and Tuesday,
Wednesday, Thursday."

"Please. No more metaphors for tonight.
Check my lungs, my sinus cavities."

"Pobrecito. Nobody wen' tell you snort sulfur
in Kona, tiptoe on sea urchins in Waikoloa,
then take Saddleback Road with one flat tire.
Que tu piensas?"

"My left foot—is it still bleeding?"

"You so funny you should go work for the State.
They hiring high school grads like Marge and Owen.

"Leave my estranged parents out of this."

"When I croaked for Maui Merwin four years ago
you think he wen' pour citric acid on me or told
me for go Arizona and start one new life? No way, José.
Him just took one good look at the gunpowder and
Albizia trees that look like one tribe of orangutans on fire,
then he wen' hole up, until *Migrations: New
and Selected Poems* came out and won one National
Book Award. But 'til this day, I still never get my ode."

                              "Don't worry, I'll mention you
                              in my next acknowledgement."

"I going be fuel for fossils by then. You know
us guys only live 'til we four then vaya con dios."

                              "I thought six."

"If I step on dog shit."

                              "Or leap over a dead rabbit."

"Como? You think we only about catching flies
under the lauhala tree? Eh, hard, you know, for be us.
The State branded us 'Invasive Species' cuz
them real estate guys wen' lose last year eleven
million dollars? And the Councilman still talking
shit about us in a public forum cuz he said if not
for us Hiromi Sato, Hilo's oldest living man,
going still have his hearing at age hundred-and-
four? 'Guilty on ninety *decibel* counts,' the morning
headline said. Decibel, what that mean?"

                              "Your song is a giant
                              garbage disposal."

"I'm the size of a freaking quarter, for Kermit's sake.
Estoy mas inocente que Free Willy, Flipper, and Jingjing,

official mascot for the Beijing Olympics. More
worse, I never ask for this side of paradise.
Chico, I was happy cuando yo era Puerto Riqueño,
speaking Spanglish, reminiscing con Ricky Martin.
But no get me wrong, este lugar no esta mal,
even though Pidgin English full of, the kind,
missing verbs like that."

                    "No predators here."

"But get citric acid, Kona coffee grains, boiling water,
the bush formerly known as brain."

                    "Can we do this when I'm insomniac?"

"No blame me for your anxiety disorder."

                    "Don't get paranoid."

"It's bad enough the Mayor tried for squeeze
his Spam musubi-shaped butt into the spotlight,
declaring one state of emergency cuz our eggs
get ninety-eight percent survival rate. How
can be our fault—that's what I like know!"

                    "Vintage Merlot."
"Huh?"

                    "My insomnia."

"Just cuz I wen' hitchhike with Wal-Mart across
the Caribbean no mean I was born yesterday."

                    "It only gets harder."

"That's the best part—the challenge
to make up more truths, muse-wrestle,
sing for the moment. I kinda like a Buddhist
that way, but not really cuz I always put out.

I more like Whitman and mirrors.
Inspiration calls, and I multiply."

                              "Need you advertise it?"

"FYI: we not in Animal Planet's top twelve noisiest.
Yes, we louder than a high-speed blender, but Google us
and we pindrops compared to blue whales, tiger pistol
shrimps, howler monkeys in the mist. But our noise manini
compared to oil spills, global warming, Karl Lagerfeld's
winter collection, dolphins committing synchronized
suicide in Japan."

                              "Tell that to the Boss."

"Who you think sent me to you?
You think I show up unannounced for fun?"

                              "But why you?"

"Cuz you maxed out on your muses.
Eleven thousand total. Many went loco.
Some joined the drug and organ trafficking business,
four switched to cosmetology, seven hundred fled
to Thailand for get sex change operation."

                              "I only wrote one book."

"I know. I read it. Not bad. Especially enjoyed
the anti-haiku:
                Mistaken for a wallaby & other rednecks
                Matilda jumped off a cliff
                Summertime."

                              "So what now?"

"You tell me; we on the same page."

II

ON BEAUTY

Gym mirrors make me feel like a deer
in *The New Yorker*: one minute it's post-
lapsarian, I'm running tête-à-tête with
Bardot or Delon or some star worth a silver
screen test, the paparazzi of Paradise
hounding us, and before I know it, I'm
down for the count, blood and earth
on my tongue, the hunter's last bullet
lodged in my gut, and all because of
what he terribly mistook for beauty.

SPLIT SECONDS

Tina-Tuna, next time Keoni squats,
Try peek on the snake squeezing his thighs.
No make obvious but look in the mirror real close.
You goin' find a phoenix tattoo rising on his trapezius.
In your wet dreams if he goin' ask you for do lateral raise with him.
Minerva Manerves already wen' do him, you know.
Only average his laka but fuzz for days.
But who cares what that has-been haggot says?
Bitch needs more than Drano for clear his throat.

So what if Keoni Born-Again?
It comes with the fellowship and the territory.
At least now he can spell E-Z-kiel.
Look at Moses "I once was bi but now I see" Kuilima from Kapalama.
Talk about poster boy for the long and winding road.
Oprah should fly his Bible-quoting ass to the Windy City.
Amazing how he went from meth to dick to Jesus to pussy
to Calvary then back to dick and meth again in one week.

Is that Kendrick Chang fighting gravity on the Gravitron.
Bet you that Shylock of Salt Lake either had one lipo
or he stay popping pills from Phuket.
Maybe it was the water in P.I.?
What? Bikram, pilates and yogilates?
I believe it. He can stretch a dollar throughout the week.

Is that a fact, Kendrick?
No wonder you're so—what's
the word?—Cirque de Soleil.

So what if his bento belly is all six-pack now
and his rectus abdominus stay rippling?
I ain't J, Mary.
I take hatha and ashtanga from Vishnu from Kenya.
I know sun salutation by heart.

I know "swadhistana" orgasm via creativity.
Besides, who goin' like top Kendrick now.
His gluteus maximus is so in-transit Gloria already.

Oh, my god, hold me back, Tina-Tuna, hold me back.
Keoni just gave me my Brokeback Mountain moment
(minus the slaughtered-sheep-in-the-pasture) for the day.
What you mean I tripping on my fantasies?
You never saw him wassup-wassup-me with his chin?
I'd kill to dream on his pectoral major right now.
Speaking of pecs, remember Larry, the Latino-looking stripper
who had threesome with Coco Canal and Tiny Bubbles?
I ran into him yesterday, acting all pee-shy in the shower.
Pah-lease, Mary, as if my George Washingtons never grazed
his midnight package at Fusion.

Oh, Jesus, Keoni coming.
Hurry, pass me the fifty-pound dumbbell.
Butch it up times ten, Mary,
Keep your vala'aus to yourself,
and no forget, your name stay Tino and not Tina or Tuna.

1968   Birthmark: Palm Sunday.

1969   Stands, wobbles, walks, trips. Daily regimen for Darwin's Olympics.

1970   Rain through the hole in a corrugated ceiling is a sensation, not yet a metaphor.

1971   First symptoms: allergic to eggs, prefers attention from strangers, entertains men from their laps.

1972   Martial Law declared. Daydreams to substitute for memories.

1973   Evelyn on the cheek—uneventful, unlike Mario, the gardener, pissing in perfect arcs.

1974   More signs: boys climbing out of bamboos in billowy skirts and chewing guava leaves for fresh wounds.

1975   Thrilla in Lethe. While maids pound dirty laundry with mallets against boulders, Mario teaches him underwater breathing exercises.

1976   Migrates to America. Longs for Mario in subtitles.

1977   Definite candidate: a look-alike for black-and-white Montgomery Clift pushing Shelley Winters off a boat.

1978   Adds to the list of likes: pepperoni pizza right between Communion and cotton candy.

1979   Camp Erdman. Lots of first bases and false alarms.

1980   Stars and sneezes, yes, but do sighs also qualify as miniature deaths?

1981   Speedos at the Y on Saturdays.

1982   Salt tasted from every corner, gives up confession.

1983   Chance encounter in a chlorinated pool: butterfly record-holder, 50 meters; fluent in Algebra and French kissing.

1984   Frotting and fear of dying increases.

1985   Music a new addition to heighten the remains of a sigh.

My Way, Your Way, No Way

Dear Mr. Paul Anka,
Barely cleared off the sludge from Typhoon Ondoy,
our streets and roads still rat-piss canals, and
The New York Times is not wasting any time
telling the world we Filipinos are back
to shooting each other in the face, out in the open,
because of a song you wrote forty years ago.
I also thought of writing your accomplices in Paris
responsible for the melody but felt some French
are better left unsaid.

What else is new?
We've been headhunting and spearing each other
since way before Lucy could walk and much after Jesus
was found hiding behind Luke in the Parable
of the Shrewd Manager. Then, when Spain,
U.S., and, for three years, Japan, invaded us,
the *mass* in *massacre*, *butch* in *butchery*, and
slaughter cut between *man* and *house* were magnified.

It's no wonder Reuters deemed us a coconut
country of contradictions. On one hand, as pastoral-
loving folks, internationally recognized for staging
a succession of snap but bullet-free revolutions;
on the other, prone to uncontrollable rage and terror—
premeditated (*juramentado*) or random (*amok*), often
resulting in trigger-happy tragedy. The cause
varies from a bruised ego, hunger, Twinkie overdose,
to an off-key note, which is why it didn't shock
me a bit, as it did millions of Manhattanites,
when I learned that the site for the latest homicide
has moved from the dark rice fields of the Philippine
Republic to the egg carton-walled karaoke bars
adorned with Christmas tree lights blinking all year long.

Can't help it, Mr. Anka,
 "My Way" is an integral part of our pop-cultural heritage,
one of our national anthems, second only to Bing Crosby's
"White Christmas." It has been since Neil Armstrong
moonwalked and a young law student, Ferdinand
Marcos, accused of shooting his father's political rival
as he was brushing his teeth, defended himself
in court and won.

In terms of statistics, "My Way" has produced
more body bags than "Making Love Out of Nothing at All,"
"Tonight I Celebrate My Love," "My Love Will Go On,"
(Theme Song from *Titanic*), and Dolly Parton's
"I Will Always Love You," simply because your song
is every Filipino man's autobiography told
with a catchy melody. Whether homesick in a foreign
soil or sick and disgusted with coups and
corruption at home, the global Pinoy finds solace,
belting out blows and regrets that, though they're
so few to mention and aren't worth a line,
dime, or rhyme, must be sung the Sinatra way—
same key, perfect intonation, no "Z's" for "C's"
("fazing the final curtain,")
no changing tenses or gender-switching,
especially at the end when it asks what is a man
and what has he got anyway?
The song is about a He, not a she, fag, dyke, chick
with a dick.

If anything, Mr. Anka, your song is prophetic.
Truly Armageddon is near, if it hasn't already come
and gone, taking with it a Jehovah's Witness
and the twelve friends he'd gunned down
after they went into hyena-hysterics at the part
about traveling each and every highway.
Oh, Mr. Anka, is your song the soundtrack
to our doom? Are we back to killing
each other—not softly—but bluntly,
the way the Marcos regime had done during

the decadent decade of martial law?

Perhaps a new song written
especially for us, Mr. Anka, will bring hope back
to the B-side of our lives. Perhaps something light,
lots of la-la-la's à la "Sing," or something sad or nostalgic
perfect for photo-ops, like "Times of Your Life,"
since we are an archipelago of ninety million smiles.
Or how about something borrowed from Tibetan monks
or inspired by Korean soap operas? Or, even better, just
make a YouTube appearance and plead to every Pinoy-
karaoke crooner slaving around the world, like Tito Ed
in Saudi Arabia, Kuya Jimmy in Milan, Papa Art hiding
in Kobe, that you're granting everyone global license
to sing "My Way" any way. I'm certain it would cut
the homicide rate in half. For now, best to postpone
your upcoming concert, as the Senate just passed a bill
boycotting your song in bars, cafés, airports,
on airwaves, and at wakes.

Federico Garcia Lorca to Be Sung in Pidgin English

Daniel Faasili,
Elvis Duldulao,
Lance Fujimura.
Them guys, they never going change:
Daniel living off of Hotel Street hookers and Samoan fairies.
Elvis, that shrimp with the FOB harelip, jackin' off
so much his palms get holes the size of saints'.
Lance, the only one who had future on his side . . .
Ho, how sad them three.

Lance,
Elvis,
Daniel.
Them guys stay burning:
Lance in Cebu City Pool Hall, chewing on squid.
Elvis in Kam Bowl, yelling at one fat-assed Gauguin model
("Eh, I said I like oxtail soup with extra ginger on the side!").
Daniel forever searching for his name
in the obit pages of the *Star Bulletin*.

Lance,
Elvis,
Daniel.
Soon six feet under:
Lance an invertebrate's wet dream.
Elvis going shit himself to death.
Daniel inside the belly of a B-52 cockroach
dog paddling across the sink of Patti's Chinese Kitchen.

Lance,
Elvis,
Daniel,
eyeing the salt on my lifelines.
They like lick 'em, that's why,
like three Siamese cats purring at one bird
of paradise under one scratch glass-eyed moon

the gods left behind.

One
By one
Bumbye.

Them guys going be wrapped up
in ti leaves and kalua'd like three little pigs;
their mothers get all goose bumps
cuz the white owls no like stop crying.

Three
Minus two
Going soon be none.

I watch them lose it halfway through "Strangers in the Night,"
singing like Sinatra, karaoke-kind, at Punani's,
and I start to think "pathetic"—no, "lonely"—
oh, shit,
did I leave the hallway light on?
Is the back door waiting for me?
How come the moon tonight one ball of pus?
What more can I do?
I wen' kill time, half of my shadow stay gone already,
and all around me,
in this watering hole,
we all waiting, falling for something, singing to someone
we don't know.

Daniel,
Elvis,
Lance,
and that gatekeeper—Myrna with the mullet—
She real bull-headed.
But sometimes she wears lipstick
false eyelashes, too.

When the microphones stop singing,
that means time for move on.

Go someplace else.
Hele on.
The ecstatic ones return to Odyssey.
The lucky ones go Manoa graveyard.
The desperate ones go Saint Thomas Square for swing on
        banyan tree branches.
That's where Daniel, Elvis, and Lance go looking for me.
But they no can find me.
They cannot?
No, they no can.
They no can.

THAT LITTLE FAGGOT DANCE

McMackin apparently pleaded with the press not to report on the slur. "I want to officially, officially apologize . . . Please don't write that statement I said as far as Notre Dame. The reason is, I don't care about Notre Dame. But I'm not a—I don't want to come out and have every homosexual ticked off at me."— Towleroad.com

Dear Coach McMackin:
I am a faggot and a homosexual and I know and am glad
you do not have a problem with either.
There really is little difference between the two,
except to distinguish the discreet from the closeted,
and when the issue extends beyond the grassy field
where preference of position is played out to a T
almost identical, but not quite, to your tight ends
and wide receivers.

       I know you were trying
to crack a joke, but it was funny only to you,
beyond boring to me, the joke being
about "that little faggot dance" that the Fighting Irish
of Notre Dame did at a night ceremony before the game,
before your boys did their own haka, beating their chests
and slapping their heads, thus losing themselves
in the Polynesian trance Hawaii fans suspect
caused them the 21-point loss.

       What I can't fathom is why
utter "faggot" at a press conference three times
then retract with, "I do not want to come out
and have every homosexual ticked off."

       Truth is, I'm not—
just as I was not offended ten years ago, when
your predecessor who got a topnotch volleyball player
pregnant refused to kick off until the name and mascot
were changed from *Rainbows* to *Warriors*,

for fear of affiliation with Newton's palette or
anything to do with meteorological phenomenon,
like the time I stood in the rain on one side
of the street and you were on the other glinting
in the tropical sunlight.

Irregardless of My Feelings

I took the risk.
Guys like him only come during a new moon.
Damage if I do, damage if I don't.
I'll cross the bridge before I get there.

Guys like him only come once.
Heartbreak-hot, jaw-dropping jaw line.
Forget the bridge, text him.
If no reply, Crayola a river.

Heartbreak-hot, dial-a-poo face.
I texted him to keep in touch.
Wait an hour then head for the river.
Flash-fantasy: soundtrack: lips-to-lips.

With bated baby's breath, I texted
Stormw8ing here.
Flash-flood warning: soundtrack: Manila winds.
Romance in disguise?

Stormw8ing. You there?
Three hours later: *Wanna cum?*
Blessing from the skies.
No holds barred.

Wanna cum over? Bring butter plz.
I second that emotion.
No hole in one.
It's whip-whip-hooray!

I second that emotion.
We summed up the storm.
Whoopeed from the neck up.
It rained hard; no one got wet.

We summed up the storm.
I took the risk irregardless of my feelings.
Bottom line: wetless.
Damage if I do, damage if I don't.

LEAKAGE

Bored with the rain boring holes in rooftops
crammed with antennas, bras and the memory
of this morning's stroll to the slaughterhouse
for markdowns on piglets, I was contemplating
a fourth-story balcony dive straight into
the tattooed back of a meth addict stacking crates
of empty Coca-Cola bottles, when the maid,
semi-recovered from swine flu she claimed
came from the communion line, broke
out of her Sunday-old quarantine to spit out
that the president's breast implants were leaking
all over the country.

Facebook verified it: "Macapal Arroyo busted
by boosted boobs." Messages flooded
my inbox with subject headings. "Tater Tits."
"Her boob-job makes ironing boards voluptuous."
"To gel or not to gel." "Oompa Loompa Strikes
Again!" "No wonder the pork barrel is empty!"
"Out: Swine Flu; In: Gloria's mosquito-
bite-size implants."

Vandals invaded my Facebook wall, a thread
of comments longer than last week's
rally. "Did she use the mole on her cheek?"
"Super Glo gets the botched job
done." "Silicone sorrows." "Sneaky cheeky
gets injected, and the country can't tell?"
"Bad booboo on boob job."
"Like they say: Leak what you sow."

Channel 2's Che Che Lazaro badgers
three witnesses in hospital scrubs—voices
warped, eyes black-barred—denying ever leaking
the leak that's now reached the front desk

of the National Bureau of Investigation
along Taft Avenue. "A discreet examination
of her implants will be conducted with utmost
sincerity," said the chief, in the same manner
as the ongoing case of the B-movie actress
who claimed the plastic surgeon made a pig
out of her—*binaboy niya ako! binaboy niya
ako!*—when he videotaped her going
down on him to the tune of "Careless Whispers"
and uploaded it onto YouTube.

The hacking-in-my-face maid leaves for confession;
boredom returns to the balcony and plunges
into bottles and tattoos, blood coursing
through labyrinths of Manila,
diluted by spit, silicone, and more rain.

ODE TO ERROR

Something as small
Something not quite

Yet seemingly gone
An *Ah*

Yesterday's banner
Mistaken for *All*

Tragic or a
Footnote to a miracle

No recollection now
Except surrendering

To error &
Other wonders

However grand
However brief.

III

Twelve Days of Christmas, Hawaiian Style

Braddah, first thing to keep in mind: it's Tutu
not true love. And the partridge part
actually is one mynah bird in one papaya tree.

Numbah two divides the coconut in half.
One for the old, other for the new.

Numbah three is for the three North Shore sistahs—
Faith, Hope, and Charity Kahanu—
who make the best spicy dried squid.

The fourth, real easy to remember.
Think four plumeria leis. Think Fab Four
from Liverpool. Think four million girls
losing their minds inside Aloha Stadium.

Five stay big and fat, like the pigs
Uncle Willie in Waialua wen' kalua with cabbage.

Six is the moon, the sun, the stars,
you, me, the Pacific blue us dream in.

Seven stay many things, good and bad.
Seven lands or seven flights.
Seven gives and seven takes.

Eight more specific—ukuleles strumming.
Try listen: G7, C7, F.

Numbah nine is us pounding poi.

Ten I know you nevah going forget.
Means pau hana time so clock out,
us go Anyplace, corner King and McCully.
Get happy hour specials. Karaoke, too.
Only cost fifty cents for every song we sing.

Eleven is the numbah of missionaries
who wen' bring twelve Salvation Army
Trinitron televisions to the islands.

As for Santa, he nevah changed.
He still imported.
Still white on the outside
but enters from front screen door now,
barefoot, and goes, "Ho, ho, ho. Aloha!"
when he passing you by in his red Datsun pickup.

New Year's Eve

for Dick Lourie

Tonight I'm charging everything
as I try to do every New Year's Eve
everything that can count as collateral:
the silver laptop that witnessed the birth

of three unpublished manuscripts
the iPod that came free with it
the blue digital camera thanks to Tim's 10%
employee discount for the transatlantic trip

the electric shaver that never fails twice
a week to give my face carpet burns
I'd donate it to Goodwill if it weren't a gift
for my 40th from an ex worth calling an ex

I'm not one to get nostalgic on pain or false starts
and if I do it's with brandy from a French monk's basement
in case ghosts of the past start colliding
with demons in the making

Charging on the bathroom sink counter
my grandfather's electric toothbrush
I will never part with
for it's worth more than a billion memories

I'd charge my phone too if I knew where it was
but knowing is too close to remembering
and the only recollection of last night
was an hour session of puking

My brother William a food-poisoning connoisseur
and tarot card reader believes it's the combination
of jet-lag, Malbec, Motrin, an empty stomach,
and insomnia

I'd dial my number again
like the hundred times
I called myself this morning
Where is Lazarus when you need him

Never mind
I'm in charge tonight
so I need to make sure the first minute
is off to a clean start

I throw the last load into the wash
I vacuum the guest room
I wipe pee spots off the porcelain rim
I shave the last five o'clock shadow of the year

I stand under the shower
for the longest time
just thinking about the books
holding my bedroom door open

books to leave for Bill, Amalia, and Brenda
books I want to carry to the far side of the world
loves and lives of role models I can afford to lose
or get stolen or chewed on by Galapagos iguanas

There's the dilemma with Bukowski
the five-ton biography of Carver
the bottle of red wine Lisa carried
all the way from London

I begin deleting one by one
the day's email messages
mostly advanced greetings from parts
of the world already a day old

From the corner of my eye
I catch it blinking
on top of the microwave
Bill must've put it there

or Gordon
or the spirit of the little girl
who runs up and down the stairs
each time the front door opens

I pick it up and dare myself
to call my sister who lives a mile from here
and is not talking to me
or my older brother to ask for a reunion rain check

or an ex to tell him to be useful
and drive me to the airport
I call my mom and I'm relieved
to hang up on her voicemail

I unload the wash and bury my face deep
into the wet wrung shirts underwear and socks
I wore for three months
in another country

I take my time and breathe
in the scent of soapy water and bleach and
now is the closest I've come so far
in my life to starting over

I put on the white shorts
bought from the bazaar in Brazil
and the white polo shirt
I got a week later

in Buenos Aires
clean white socks
with a hole in the right big toe
as I listen to the voice on the radio

counting down to the top song
of the dying year
then I walk out
every light in the guesthouse switched on

guiding me through
all the smoke
one hand not letting go
of my black suitcase

and its four worn wheels
the other deep into
all the emptiness
my small pocket can hold.

REUNION

for Jessica Hagedorn and Ching Valdes

Before Jessica sent back the chicken,
the black widow dropped by to show
off her latest husband. Then Ching arrived
bringing the latest typhoon body count
from the motherland we sometimes call
home. When the chicken returned, Jessica
was already done dreaming of Lorca
mingling with moths and stars. I kept on
and on about sleep-deprived evenings
in the Hamptons hitting me so hard it felt
like ten thousand vigils. Then Ching
said: Life's too short, we really should find
tables for more times like this.

TENTH GRADE SONNET

No matter what, I like him still be mine
even though the worst I already know
goin' only be more worse and look more
pathetic come cafeteria time
when April bitches to me about how
after all the pep talks she gave, I no
like accept the fact he wen' go outgrow
our kisses. This so hard I like die now.
Shit, I think I losing it. But maybe
not, cuz I stay hurting and so hoping,
meaning I know I not imagining
loneliness yet. Whatever already!
But still yet. He my guardian angel,
the one making my dreams perfect as hell.

How to Get Anderson Cooper to Take Notice

Do a quick one-eighty.
Stock up on Evian and Eveready.
Be on standby should fate dry up Anderson's voice
inside a dusty war-bound bus as his flashlight suddenly
fades in the darkness of a massacre.
As fate will be fate, you and he will meet
at a PEN Conference.
Nadine Gordimer will be the common denominator.
Zen him right away.
Smile. Do not audition for his attention.
Invite him to your pocket garden
surrounded by bougainvilleas and maids.
Do not resurrect Rwanda, frozen spaghetti, or the pet snake
that once lived in the grotto with the Virgin Mary.
Allude to the kiss imported from New Haven.
Share your expertise on the contradiction-filled word "Aloha,"
where one's love is another's goodbye.
Tell him what it's really like to be CEO of Haiku Dot Com.
Good segue into the subject of poetry and concubinage,
singling out Yu Hsuan-Chi from mid-ninth century,
how poetry and banishment by a jealous lover
had left her homeless.
Quickly make an excuse
to disappear so as to reappear
with a box of truffles, cognac, and—conducted by moonlight,
Joao Gilberto on the guitar—sing "Desafinado"
slightly out of tune.
Under a star-stricken night, give back
the garden to the dream and watch how everything
in darkness falls perfectly into place.

GOOGLING AFTER BEING ATTACKED BY THE HEART OF AMERICA

1.

bangungot = *bangon* (to rise) + *ungol* (moaning).

2.

dinuguan: pig entrails cooked in pig's blood.
pakbet: mixed vegetables—eggplants, okra, string beans, squash, tomatoes, garlic, onions—with pork and shrimp paste.
sizzling sisig: chopped parts of a pig's cheeks, ears, snout, brain.
adobo: pork (or chicken) marinated in oil, vinegar, soy sauce (Silver Swan, preferably); garlic, and pepper.
ox brain: served fried, with kalamansi.
chicharon: vat-fried pork served with a bowl of vinegar and San Miguel or Red Horse beer.

Recipes for high blood pressure, gout, increased libido, and nightmares otherwise known as *bangungot*.

3.

In Hawaii, between 1937 and 1948, eighty-four Filipino men, between ages twenty and forty, died mysteriously in their sleep. Honolulu pathologists were baffled. Dr. Alvin V. Majoska, a part-Hawaiian coroner, caused panic and mass hysteria among islanders when he published his headline-making "Nightmare Deaths" report in 1948, noting only Filipinos were the victims of this unknown disease. All were migrant plantation laborers. All were healthy. No signs of foul play. Autopsy findings: a swollen heart, massive fluid in lungs, bleeding pancreas, abdominal cavity still contained semi-digested meals. Pathologists attributed the deaths to acute hemorrhagic pancreatitis, presumably caused by Filipino diet rich in sodium, cholesterol, and uric acid.

When it became apparent that Filipinos were the only ones dying mysteriously in their sleep, Korean, Portuguese, Puerto Rican, and other plantation laborers used the double armor of paranoia and scapegoating to protect themselves against the killer nightmare. The Japanese and Chinese who had already left the camps to set up their private businesses in the capital were also not immune to such phobias. Hatred, fear, ignorance leapfrogged from island to island, countryside to townside. Folks went to sleep without eating or ate without sleeping. Sleep with a Filipino and you would never dream in this world again.

Filipinos lost their jobs or their insurance premiums went up. Suspicious glares, racial epithets, rumbles in the fields under the blue heated sky, solidifying Hawaii's racial divisiveness and perpetuating negative stereotypes of Filipinos as strikebreakers, flat-nosed sexual predators, carriers of TB, hepatitis-B virus, and a mysterious ailment that, in the West, has come to be known as Sudden Unexpected Death Syndrome, or SUDS.

4.

Sorry, Sam, but New York City just bought the last
of the chicharons. You can try Jinky's Filipinoy.
Is that—what's the word? redundant?—on North
King Street though I doubt you'll find anything
there anymore, except dust mites or the last bar
of extra-strength skin-whitening soap. What
a shame Marie had to make that left turn onto
the front steps of Pagoda Hotel and catch Nanding
smooching with that puta Emme. Their sari-sari
store/travel agency/door-to-door balikbayan box
delivery/money remittance services looked
very promising pa naman.

Forget wasting your steps on Phil-Mart. Otherwise,
I would've suggested it to you, since it's only—how
do you say it?—a hop then a skip then a jump away?
Alicia should just donate that sign to Goodwill; it's
a—whatchamacallit?—misdenomer. The last time

she sold pork rinds fireworks were still legal.
Thought she stopped selling because she converted
to Islam, but turned out she was only courting
a millionaire-turned-vegetarian with B.O.

Just drive over to Manang Mercy's kalamansi-
green store at the end of Kaumualii Street, right across
Kalakaua Intermediate School where the Pumping
Iron Cops were filmed taking turns bashing,
Rodney King-style, Thelma's middle son
for getting kindergarteners hooked on meth.
I think Mercy still has a bag or two left of chicharon,
Unless she's Federal Expressed them already
to her four sons—all doctors, still single,
would you believe?—I'm sure she suspects what
everyone's already confirmed. But I cannot lie:
her store is the only one with a working freezer
west of the State Capitol. It's exploding
with buckets of pig's blood, goat stew, milkfish
stuffed with raisins and diced potatoes, and
a towering stack of peppery-garlicky sausages
she especially ordered from Sampaguita's Sausage
Factory and DVD Rentals and feeds to Ermo
and five Japanese elderlies she also caregives for
whenever their cholesterol, uric acid, and blood pressure
stabilize, or whenever she wants to relive
what the Imperial Army did to her hometown
of Vigan, Ilocos Sur, morning of February 12, 1945.

5.

In 1977, at the height of the Marcos dictatorship, the filmmaker Kidlat
Tahimik made a movie about the nightmares of a jeepney driver and called
it Mababangong Bangungot (*Perfumed Nightmares*). He screened it at the
Berlin Film Festival, where it took home the International Critics Prize.

6.

Dinuguan = pig entrails + blood = Martial Law = nightmares + a jeepney driver = film festivals + Madame Imelda Marcos's Major Complex = a burial in progress = Ferdinand Marcos in a glass sarcophagus + wax = a Bach requiem.

ALMOST

It's almost ready.
If you don't believe, look.

Chair, though backless,
Now has a red seat.

Add two more legs
And—voilà—a table.

Meanwhile, steel and aluminum
Are slowly shining

Into pots and pans.
Silver, on the other hand,

Is still undecided—
Fork? Spoon? Ladle? All?

Halfway-bed, however,
Can no longer be mistaken

For just another corner
With a floating form.

Breakfast, unfortunately,
Remains a foreign word.

But not for long.
Like coffee and the rest

Of the morning's cast
In this room

Growing closer
And closer to memory.

70

On Silence

Is it the Garcia Lorca kind
faithful as a cricket's
tune about a boy fishing
in a pool of rainwater
for his lost voice
praying it'll sing back
so he can wear it
on his finger again
like a wedding ring?

Maybe it's the anti-parakeet
Nicanor Parra kind
remorseful as a memoir
that survived four wars
half a dozen sexually
transmitted depressions
insomnia-
inspired hallucinations
and a dedication to
its remaining readers
last count forty-five
asking them to burn each page
upon reading memories
it had tried to capture

unless it's the Paz kind
not Paz-be-with-you of olden
days difficult now
to digest Paz or any Zense
of peace without Belano or Bolaño
pearly-gate-crashing in an Impala
slingshooting saints out
of their poses harping
on angels reciting bad poetry
aloud anything to disturb

the last of the angry gods'
siesta atop a mountain of ashes
once rich without meaning.

EPITHALAMION

Beloved, as you and I stand face-to-face
on reclamation land littered with yesterday's
luau, just a block away from the HIV
testing center where the island runs to
when it's run out of condoms, lube,
and instant coffee and, four blocks from there,
the bookmobile I loved disappearing
into, until you found me on MySpace,
my head at two-thirty tilt, my smile
fuller than a Cherry Blossom contestant,
the way I'm smiling now, at us, and
squinting, too, from too much sun
and not enough wind, as Tina, ordained
minister through the Internet and certified
by State of Hawaii, declares you
and me officially man and groom,
while your mom and my mom,
who beat the alarm to pencil her eyebrows,
shed tears with your grandma and Sue,
envy of fat fags and hags. They ditched
lunch to be with us. Yama, too, friend from
Day One, and Auntie Rose and Uncle Mike
who took the first flight out of North Carolina
to eat Spam and be wedding witnesses,
and my dad in the wheelchair, fighting
for his right leg. Even Auntie Mari has
skipped water aerobics so she can snap
her granddaughter Malina out of her flower
girl role. Except for your dad and my
dearest friend Glenn who saved me
when I couldn't, and, oh, yeah, Zack,
who is not dead but constipated in Buenos
Aires from too much steak, perfect
attendance otherwise for rice shower
and I do's. And should this faithful day

turn health into hell, or time run us over,
or you go ballistic because of my self-
made millionaire gimmicks; in other words,
should you decide to take off with the good
times and leave me with love alone, I will
take it, as I take you now with this vow,
on this day of refuge and reclamation,
when happiness and eternity,
mine and ours, are one again.

VIGIL

11:57 a.m. A bus terminal outside Madrid's Mendez Alvaro metro station, he waits with a one-way ticket to Mojacar, home to Spaghetti Westerns like *Marcha o Muere*, and *Treasure Island* with Orson Welles as Long John Silver.

Mojacar: home for the next month, with cacti, lemon and orange groves for neighbors.

Blood, like sakura petals, blossoms on a crumpled napkin.

Biting one's lip is no accident. Filipinos believe it means someone is remembering you as though you were already dead.

The deeper the gash, the more vivid the memory.

Over beer and platitas of tortillas on toothpicks, Filipinos conversing in Spanish-Tagalog.

Espangalog? Tagañol?

In Spanish there are two ways of being: *ser*, permanent, for poets, and *estar*, temporary, for when one is ill or waiting. In Tagalog, there is no *to be* verb.

Keep digressions out of the conversation, and you ostracize 99% of Filipinos.

12:28 p.m. A seventeen-year-old memory of Madrid:

"I told you to stay in London" —his Brit bf.

"I got bored waiting."

"You can't stay here. Alison's parents—"

"Fuck London, fuck your homophobic friends."

Fortunately for him, Filipinos, who make up the largest Asian group in Spain—90% of them are women working as maids—believe in the "mi casa es tu casa" code.

He ran into Lani at Plaza de Chueca, 3 a.m., managed to vent without disclosing his sexual preferences or talking about how love had gone through more break-up/make-up cycles than one of Edward Albee's couples.

"What a dump!"—Martha.

Lani offered him the studio apartment she and her boyfriend rented; it was their weekend love nest.

Ring on her finger told another story.

Next day, Lani's boyfriend, accompanied by another woman, and mistaking him for a vagabond in boxer shorts, nearly killed him.

Lani's boyfriend gestured at him to put his money away; a tight lip insured him free lodging.

Over chocolate con churros, the only meaning he could squeeze out from his year-old relationship with Joseph:

"Who's afraid of Virginia Woolf?"—George.

"I am, George, I am."—Martha.

First major symptom of doom: a phone call from an American Express agent.

"Yes, Sir, cut the card in half. Yes, Sir, now."

2:55 p.m. Window seat #5, next to an old woman with a gummy smile.

3:50 p.m. Miles of dry earth like
skin of dying lions next
exit: Ikea.

Nineteen hours ago, he was in Newark with Robyn and Allan, chain-eating Swedish meatballs.

"I sleep on IKEA, I eat on IKEA, I think on IKEA"—Robyn.

"When do they find time to furnish the world, they only have the sun for three months."—Allan.

He misses? Allan, Robyn, Swedish meatballs, massage, and ABBA.

Honey, if you change
Your mind I'll be first in line
Take a chance on me
        —ABBA haiku

5:00 p.m. "Death laid eggs in the wound"—Garcia Lorca.

5:45 p.m. A hilly, whitewashed pueblo and an overdeveloped playa make up the centerfold of Mojacar's tourist brochure.

Every four years, Rio de Agua, the pueblo's river, touches water.

8:29 p.m. The route to Lorca's death, as described by his biographer Ian Gibson in *The Assassination of Federico Garcia Lorca*, was a five-mile march that began in front of the Archbishop Moscoco's palace and ended under an olive tree, on the edge of Alfacar, Viznar.

Lorca's comrades that August night: Dioscoro Galindo Gonzalez, a one-legged schoolteacher, and two bullfighters, Joaquin Arcollas Cabezas and Francisco Galadi Mergal.

Ainadamar: Arabic for "Fountain of Tears."

"Here all I want is wide-open eyes
to see that body that can never rest"—Lorca.

"Wait a while / Till a little moonbeam comes peeping through"—
Billie Holiday crooning despite the iPod battery icon glowing red.

12:45 a.m. Ivan Morris, in his introduction to *The Pillow Book of Sei Shonagon*: "I have however, preferred to retain the confused time-sequence of the traditional texts"

"I have however, preferred to retain the confused time-sequence of the traditional texts"

"not because this was necessarily the order"

"necessarily the order in which she arranged her book, but because"

"in which . . . because any systematic reorganization"

"arranged her book, but because any systematic reorganization"

"reorganization would be arbitrary"

"arbitrary and possibly"

"arbitrary and possibly"

"any systematic reorganization"

"confused time she arranged her book because systematic organization would be arbitrary and possibly misleading"

3:04 a.m. Sleep interrupted. Bergman's *Hour of the Wolf*, when nightmares play in slow motion.

"The soul, without the body, plays"—Petronius.

Hour of unforgiveness.

3:33 a.m. The memory of Ireneo Funes shines upon him. A Borges creation, Funes was paralyzed after getting thrown by a wild horse. The accident reduced him to days and insomniac nights in a room with unlit candles, staring out at a fig tree, examining cobwebs, contemplating the sunset, remembering in English, French, Portuguese, and Latin.

"My memory, sir, is like a garbage disposal"—Funes.

How many faces does a dead man wear throughout his wake?

In lieu of sleep, he busied himself instead with memories—his and not his—like being hounded in a dream with one eye open.

The Idea

You'd think we would've gotten used
to it by now since all we ever seem
to do is turn breath and blood
into memory. But we always want
what is not ours, making time for
hunger, even after the realization
that Oh, shit, we've been here before,
why are we still shaking?
How did we stand still, breathe
and bleed for the slaughter
we weren't meant for?

NOTES

"Twelve Short Takes on Montgomery Clift" could not have been written without Patricia Bosworth's amazing biography *Monty*.

* * *

I wrote "That Little Faggot Dance" in response to the August 2009 incident at a Western Athletic Conference meeting where the University of Hawaii football coach used a gay slur. The poem, with an epigraph from Towleroad. com where I first read about the incident, appeared a week later in *Honolulu Weekly*.

* * *

The following poems in Pidgin were inspired by and modeled after:

"A True Account of Talking to a Coqui Frog at Reed Island, Hilo": Frank O'Hara's "A True Account of Talking to the Sun on Fire Island."

"Federico Garcia Lorca to Be Sung in Pidgin English": Garcia Lorca's "Fable of Three Friends to Be Sung in Rounds."

"Tenth Grade Sonnet": Shakespeare's "Sonnet 147."

"Irregardless of My Feelings": O'Hara's "In Memory of My Feelings."

GRATEFUL ACKNOWLEDGMENTS

Mahalo nui loa to the editors of the following journals and on-line magazines, in which earlier versions of some of these poems first appeared:

Bamboo Ridge, Chain, Court Green, EOAGH, Hanging Loose, Honolulu Weekly, Sunday Inquirer Magazine, The North American Review, The Philippine Free Press, and *Tinfish.*

"Twelve Short Takes on Montgomery Clift," "Federico Garcia Lorca To Be Sung in Pidgin English," "Twelve Days of Christmas, Hawaiian Style," "Tenth Grade Sonnet, and "Googling After Being Attacked by the Heart of America" are from the chapbook *The Filipino Exiled Poet Channels Montgomery Clift & Other Poems*, published by 2nd Avenue Press.

This book would not have been possible without the support and encouragement from my family—my brothers Gus and William, my sister Ghel, our mom Cecilia, and my brother-in-law Greg Boorsma; Allan Punzalan Isaac, Jeffrey Rebudal, Jessica Hagedorn, Karen Tei Yamashita, Lucy Mae San Pablo Burns & Anjali Arondekar, Paul & Hyon Chu Yi-Toguchi, Bill Maliglig & Gordon Wong, Noel Madlansacay, Wilma Consul, Robyn Magalit Rodriguez, Marissa Diccion-Ocreto, David Blackmore, Leonel Guzman, and Mike Santos for offering me their homes away from home; Jae & Delan Robillos, Christine Balance; David Azama, The Pukis; Amalia Bueno, Tim Peterson, Craig Santos Perez, Rigoberto Gonzalez, and especially to Paolo Javier, who took time off from his poetry manuscript to help polish mine; and maraming maraming salamat to the magnificent gang at Hanging Loose Press—Bob Hershon, Marie Carter, Donna Brook, and my editors Mark Pawlak and Dick Lourie for giving shine, love, and other vigils to my poetry.